A First Look at Art

Celebrations

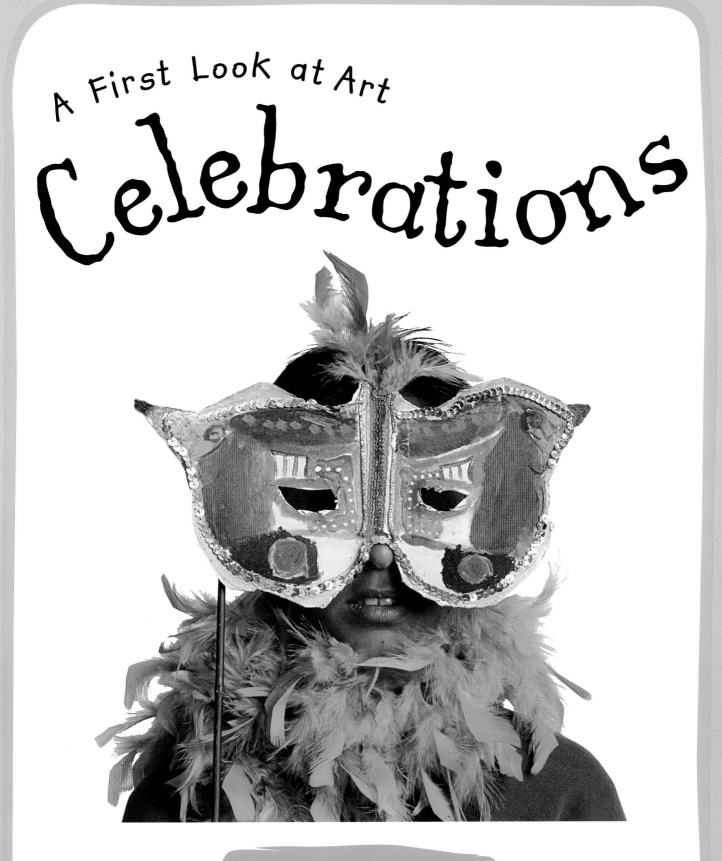

Ruth Thomson

Chrysalis Children's Books

First published in the UK in 2005 by
Chrysalis Children's Books
An imprint of Chrysalis Books Group Plc
The Chrysalis Building, Bramley Road
London W10 6SP

ISBN 1 84458 197 7

British Library Cataloguing in Publication Data for this
book is available from the British Library.

Editorial manager *Joyce Bentley*
Project manager *Rasha Elsaeed*
Editor *Susie Brooks*
Designers *Rachel Hamdi, Holly Mann*
Picture researcher *Claire Gouldstone*
Photographer *Jerry Moeran*
Consultant *Erika Langmuir, formerly Head of Education,
The National Gallery, London, UK*

The author and publishers would like to thank the
following people for their contributions to this book:
Sue Jameson, Jean Harrison and pupils at Church
Cowley St James Primary School, Oxford.

Printed in China

Typography *Natascha Frensch*
Read Regular, READ SMALLCAPS and Read Space;
European Community Design Registration 2003 and
Copyright © Natascha Frensch 2001-2004 Read Medium,
Read Black and *Read Slanted* Copyright © Natascha
Frensch 2003-2004

READ™ is a revolutionary new typeface that will
enchance children's understanding through clear, easily
recognisable character shapes. With its evenly spaced and
carefully designed characters, READ™ will help children
at all stages to improve their literacy skills and is ideal for
young readers, reluctant readers and especially children
with dyslexia.

...ction of content has
...are of any unintentional
...ecessary corrections

...of Deborah Weil,
...003, Digital Image,
...llie P. Bliss Bequest
...n des Musées
...ndon 2004. 10-11
...eque des musees de la
...on 200... 10-19 Reproduced by the
kind permission of the Earl and Countess of Harewood and Trustees of the Harewood
House Trust. 22 Corbis/© Charles & Josette Lenars. 23 Corbis/© Charles & Josette
Lenars. 26 The Art Archive/Mireille Vautier. 27 Photographs by Neil Thomson,
sculptures courtesy of Deborah Weil, The Mexico Gallery, London.

Contents

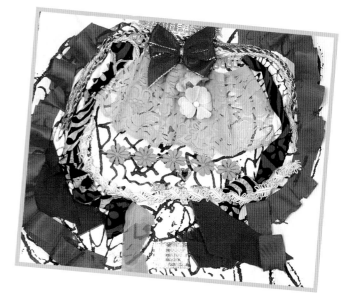

TIME TO CELEBRATE

Birthday, *Marc Chagall, 1915*
(80.6 x 99.7 cm)

Celebrations are ideal subjects for artists. Whether they honour a happy event – such as a birth – or a particular time – such as New Year – they are usually full of colour and excitement. In this book you'll see how celebrations have inspired different artists. There are questions to help you look at the images in detail, and also ideas for creating your own festive works of art.

◉ *You'll find answers to the questions and information about the artists on pages 30-31.*

Arty tips

✩ Look out for Arty tips boxes that suggest handy techniques and materials to use in your own work.

Floating feeling

Chagall painted his intimate picture *(left)* not only to celebrate the birthday of his fiancée Bella, but also to show how much he loved her. To express his bliss, he portrayed himself floating in the air, reaching round with an impossibly long neck to kiss his future wife. She leans forward on tiptoes to respond, holding up the birthday bouquet her sweetheart has given her.

Fluttering flags

Monet's picture *(right)* depicts the hubbub and flurry of a national festival in France. The bird's-eye view down a long Paris street shows a hectic blur of moving figures, surrounded by fluttering *tricolores* (the three-coloured French flags). Monet was more interested in capturing the patterns of light and colour than in showing clear details of the event — but his quick brushstrokes give a sense of the excitement of the day.

Rue Montorgueil, Paris, Festival of **30 June**, *1878*
Claude Monet
1878
(81 x 50 cm)

Picture hunt

✦ Picture hunt boxes suggest other artists and artworks that you might like to look at.

The first celebration in people's lives usually takes place when they're born. This picture celebrates two births and several amazing coincidences.

◉ *Guess how the two ladies are related.*
◉ *Can you spot at least five differences between them?*
◉ *What is strange about their situation?*

The gold writing in the bottom left-hand corner of the picture explains who the two women are:

Two Ladies of the
    Cholmondeley Family,
Who were born the same day,
Married the same day,
And brought to Bed the same day.

The
Cholmondeley
Ladies
*Unknown British
artist
c1600–1610
(88.9 x
172.7 cm)*

Wrapped up well

Notice how stiff and straight the babies are. This is because they were swaddled (tightly wrapped up). They are wearing elaborate christening gowns over their swaddling clothes.

◉ *What do you notice about the patterns on their christening robes?*

Crisp colours

The artist used a narrow range of colours in this picture. The minutely drawn details of the women's grand, decorative clothes help them to stand out against the plain pillows behind.

◉ What are the main colours used?
◉ What effect do the red shawls have?

FAMILY PATTERNS

Joshua, aged 9

Matching mum

The patterns on the clothes of each Cholmondeley lady and her baby were special to the families of their husbands.

Invent a pattern of your own for a mother and her new baby.

◉ Draw the outlines of a mum and baby.

◉ Add busy patterns to their clothes.

◉ Colour them in so they match.

Olivia, aged 9

Leighia, aged 9

Robert, aged 7

Picture hunt

✿ Discover the work of Mary Cassatt, who often painted mothers and babies. Look also at **Mother Roulin with her Baby** by Vincent van Gogh; **Mother and Child** by Jan Steen; and any pictures of the **Virgin and Child**.

Collage clothing

Create a collage from your clothing pattern.

◉ Enlarge a patterned section of your mother and baby drawing on a photocopier.

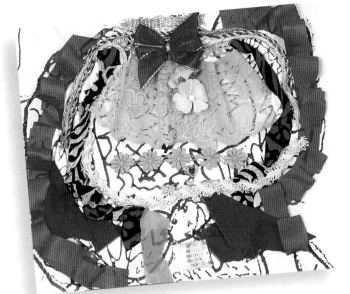

A group of children, all aged 8

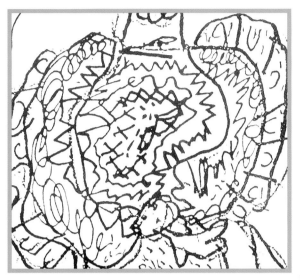

Leighia, aged 9

◉ Gather pieces of lace, shiny scraps of fabric, sequins, beads, bows, scrumpled tissue, ribbon, ric-rac and other colourful trimmings. Stick them on to your pattern, using PVA glue.

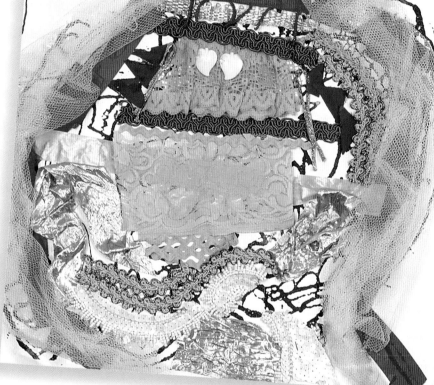

A group of children, all aged 8

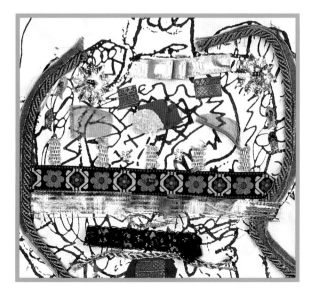

A group of children, all aged 8

Arty tips

✧ Repeat patterns can be effective. Try taking a shape that you like and repeating it in rows. Experiment by using different colours and textures for each row.

✧ You could put your collage on a greetings card, maybe for a new baby or a birthday.

FEASTING AND FUN

The villagers in this action-packed scene are celebrating St George's Day, in memory of the brave legendary knight. St George was said to have rescued a beautiful princess by killing a dragon that was about to devour her.

◉ *Can you spot two villagers acting out the story of St George?*
◉ *Where else is St George pictured?*

Double celebration

St George's Day was a religious festival that took place late in April. The people here are also using the opportunity to celebrate the arrival of spring.

◉ *Discover:*
• *a group of men sword-dancing*
• *men wrestling*
• *people eating and drinking*
• *players with balls and bats*
• *two children riding a hobby horse*
• *some musicians*
• *a group of children following a jester (in a red-and-yellow outfit)*
• *a stage with spectators*
• *men and women dancing*
• *people who are not having fun – what are they doing?*

Kept apart

Although the painting is busy, the artist has separated all the different activities. None of the scenes overlap, so we see each part clearly.

◉ *What are the two most important buildings?*
◉ *What clue shows that the villagers are farmers?*

A Carnival on the Feast Day
of St George in a Village
near Antwerp
Abel Grimmer
1605
(42 x 66.7 cm)

Repeating red

Notice that the artist has painted many villagers with either a hat, skirt, top or trousers in bright red. These repeating red details help your eyes dance across the picture. They also unite the village.

◉ *What else can you see that's red?*

CELEBRATING SCHOOL

A fabulous frieze

Celebrate life at your school by making a huge collage frieze about it.

◉ Place the school building at the centre.

◉ Include interesting landmarks from the local village, town or city.

◉ Cut out and colour separate figures doing activities that happen at your school. Use the ideas shown here to help you.

◉ Glue everything in place.

✧ after-school activities and clubs

The whole school, aged 5-11

✧ camps and outings

✧ playground equipment and hobbies

✧ fundraising events, such as a cake or sweet stall

✧ dancing, plays and other shows

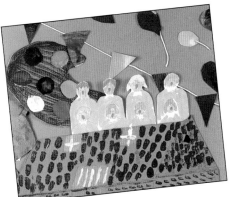

✧ special events, such as fêtes and open days

✧ local important buildings or other typical sights

✧ your school badge or emblem

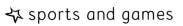

✧ sports and games

Picture hunt

✧ Look at pictures of outdoor festivities such as **Independence Centenary** by Henri Rousseau; **A Village Fête in Honour of St Hubert and St Anthony** by Pieter Breughel the Younger, and **V. E. Day Celebrations** by L. S. Lowry.

A Festival of Electricity (detail), *Raoul Dufy, 1937 (mural 10 x 60 m; 250 panels – each 200 x 120 cm)*

Whoosh! In this explosive picture a fairy figure streaks through a night sky, caught in the blaze of a dazzling searchlight. She symbolises the marvel of electricity, bringing light and uniting the world with her magnificent arrival.

A massive mural

Dufy painted this scene as part of a huge mural decorating the Palace of Light at the Paris International Exhibition of 1937. It is probably the biggest painting in the world.

⊙ *How has Dufy symbolised different parts of the world in his painting?*

Electrical invention

Along the base of the mural, Dufy traced steps in the discovery of electricity, with portraits of scientists and other important figures. Many of them stand beside their inventions.

⊙ *The scientists and other figures are named. Who can you spot in this section of the mural?*

Seeing the light

Along the top of the mural, Dufy celebrated the effects and benefits of electric light. Notice the way he has painted the different sorts of light with splodges, lines, dots or squiggles. They give a feeling of gaiety and rejoicing.

⊙ *How has Dufy made the lights stand out?*

LIGHTS AT NIGHT

Sparkling skies

If your school or home computer has a drawing and painting package, experiment with different media and marks to create some light pictures like these.

Sarah, aged 11

Zoe and Michelle, both aged 11

Hayder and Tom, both aged 11

Joshua, aged 10

Anne, aged 11

Amber and Kitty, both aged 10

◉ If you don't have a computer, you can create similar effects with paint. Use spots, splashes, lines and wiggles, just like Dufy did.

Picture hunt

✧ Look at other pictures that celebrate electric lighting, such as **Battle of Lights, Coney Island – Mardi Gras,** by Joseph Stella; **New York Night** and **The Radiator Building at Night,** both by Georgia O'Keeffe.

Dancing lights

Try spatter-painting on some paper to imitate Dufy's light effects.
- ◉ Dip your brush in runny paint.
- ◉ Flick your wrist to make blobs and trails across the paper.
- ◉ Using several bright colours, criss-cross paint all over the paper.

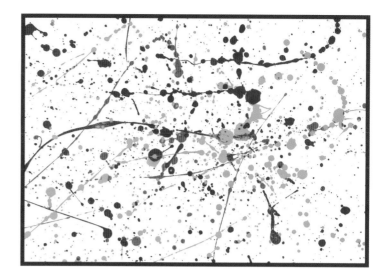

Leo, aged 6

Nailah, aged 6

Kada, aged 6

Arty tips

☆ Spatter-painting is messy, so wear an apron and cover both your work table and the floor before you start. If possible, paint outside.

☆ For fine dots, dip a toothbrush in paint and flick the bristles with your finger (keep the bristles pointing away from you).

Crazy connections

Create a picture to show how people connect with one another around the world today.

Sangeeta, aged 11

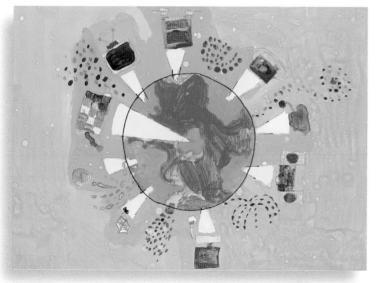

Louise, aged 11

- ◉ Perhaps you might draw a globe or a map of the world.
- ◉ Think of communications devices, such as the telephone, television, computers and the Internet. Decide how to show these in your picture.

A GLORIOUS GOAL

The footballer takes aim, kicks and yes – it's a goal! In this busy picture of a football match, the artist records very clearly how the winners, losers and onlookers react to a goal being scored.

All in the action

The poses of the figures tell the story. Two players on the winning team are hugging; some throw their arms up in the air, whooping and jumping for joy. The spectators join in, some clapping and one waving a rattle.

◉ *How does the expression of the goal scorer differ from the rest of his team?*

◉ *How would you describe the postures, expressions and gestures of the losers?*

Goal, *William Roberts, 1968 (152 x 123 cm)*

What a feeling!

Roberts did not try to paint the players here as individuals. They all look alike, with similar faces, solid bodies, tubular arms and legs and cap-like hair. What the artist most wanted to depict were the contrasting feelings of triumph and disappointment.

◉ *How do the team colours convey the players' moods?*

High drama

The artist distorted the shape and size of the pitch and goal-posts, and bunched the players together. These tricks create a dramatic effect.

◉ *Why might Roberts have added the extra lines and goal-posts?*
◉ *Why did Roberts include the three photographers?*

WINNERS AND LOSERS

Photographic fun

Have fun with your friends taking photographs of sporting moments. Contrast winners and losers in the same shot. How will you show which is which? Think carefully about how to pose people:

◉ Who will be the main focus of the photograph – the winner or the loser?

◉ What props might a winner hold – a cup, medal, badge, rosette or other prize?

Curtis, aged 11

Inido and Trephy, both aged 11

◉ What gesture might a winner make? How about the loser?

◉ Will you take the photo close up or from further away?

◉ Will you ask people to look towards or away from the camera?

Curtis, Emma and Max, all aged 11

◉ Try putting a mirror in your composition, to create unusual effects.

Picture hunt

✧ Compare other pictures of football games, such as **Footballers at the Parc des Princes** by Nicholas de Staël; or **Football Players** by Henri Rousseau.

✧ Look at the way Norman Rockwell depicted people's feelings at a baseball game in **The Dugout.**

Striking sculptures

Make a model of a winner or a loser.

◉ Bend and twist lengths of garden wire into the shape of a figure.

◉ Think how people look when they are upset or disappointed. Show their sadness in their pose – they might hunch their shoulders, hang their head, curl up or slump in a heap.

Matthew, aged 10

Connor, Jack and Marko, all aged 9

◉ Imagine how a winner might pose – perhaps with the head thrown back, the chest puffed out, both arms open wide or hands clasped high.

◉ Wrap the wire with bubble wrap to give your figure muscles. Stick this in place with masking tape.

◉ Cover the bubble wrap and tape with a layer of mod-roc.

◉ When the figure is dry, paint it – clothed or plain – then varnish it with PVA. Alternatively, make some clothing out of fabric scraps.

Zoe and Christina, both aged 11

Arty tips

✫ To suggest success or failure, concentrate on the pose and gesture of your figure and ignore the face.

✫ If you want your figure to stand upright, exaggerate the size of its feet.

CARNIVAL PARADE

Once a year – in places such as Trinidad in the Caribbean, Rio de Janeiro in Brazil, and New Orleans in America – thousands of people celebrate the carnival. Streets come alive with dancers dressed in dazzling costumes, swaying to rhythmic music in front of excited crowds.

Colourful costumes

People spend weeks making costumes like these, decorated with feathers, bright paint and sometimes sparkling sequins. Some people also make huge papier mâché wings or tails.

◉ *What do you notice about the decoration of the costume above?*

Notting Hill
Carnival
Costume
*London, UK
1980s/1990s*

Amazing masks

Many people wear playful or gruesome masks to hide their identity as they party through the carnival. Lively masked parades are a spectacular sight. The masks are often decorated with objects that have a particular meaning. Feathers, for example, are a symbol of being able to rise above difficulties and grow spiritually.

Bobbing bird

Most carnival masks, such as this one of a bird (*right*), are made by bending wire into a frame and then covering it with papier mâché.

◉ *What strikes you first about this mask?*
◉ *What part of the bird does the face mask form?*
◉ *How does the rest of the person's costume also resemble a bird?*

Bienne-Lez-Happart Carnival Costume, *Belgium, c1997*

23

DAZZLING DISGUISES

Marvellous masks

Make an amazing mask to wear, so nobody will recognise you.

⊙ Draw a mask shape with large eyeholes on card and cut it out. Cut out the eyeholes as well.

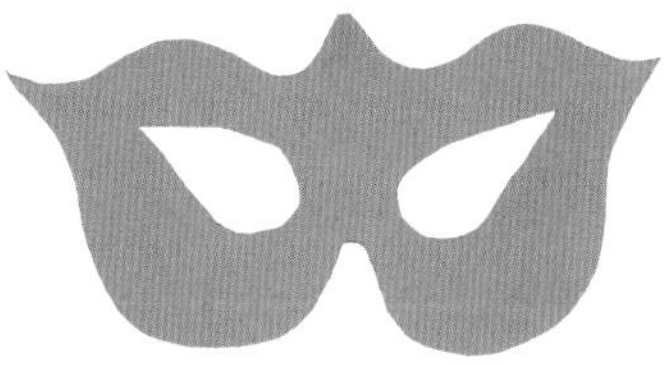

⊙ Paint the mask in strong, glowing colours.

Joshua, aged 9

⊙ Glue on sparkly sequins, glittery beads and coloured feathers. Add extra patterns with a gold or silver pen.

⊙ Tape a stick to the back of the mask so you can hold it up.

All the masks on this page were made in art club, by children aged 8–11

Modelled by Louise, aged 11

Modelled by Mark, aged 11

Modelled by Louise, aged 11

Modelled by Arun, aged 11

Picture hunt

☆ Look at carnival costumes in pictures such as **Mardi Gras** by Paul Cézanne; **A Carnival Night** by Henri Rousseau or **A Carnival Scene** by Giambattista Tiepolo.

☆ Look at paintings featuring masks, such as **Masks** by James Ensor or **Musicians in Masks** by Pablo Picasso.

Cool costumes

Design an extraordinary costume to wear at a carnival parade.

Chloe,
aged 10

Adele,
aged 10

Jade,
aged 10

Freaky faces

Make a model mask to hang on your wall or door.

Viv, aged 10

Martha, aged 10

◉ Model a fantastic face in self-hardening clay.

◉ Once the clay is dry, paint it in striking colours.

◉ Cut a piece of stiff card. Paint it in contrasting colours to your mask.

Gina,
aged 10

Hannah,
aged 10

Taniska and Megan,
aged 10

Martha,
aged 10

Greta, aged 10

◉ Glue the mask on to the card.

◉ If you make several masks, you could display them by sticking them inside a decorated shoebox.

Skeleton
Decorated
with Animal
and Plant
Forms
Felipe Linares
1992
(life-size)

On the first two days of November, Mexicans celebrate their most important festival – The Day of the Dead. Families remember relatives who have died, but it is not a sad or spooky occasion. The festival is treated as a celebration of life. It is a time of great happiness and humour.

The living dead

Some Mexican artists have become famous for making huge papier mâché skeletons. The one on the left shows the Mexicans' belief in the renewal of life after death. New leaves and branches sprout from the skeleton's bony joints, and flowers twine around its limbs and chest. It is also a home for wildlife.

◉ *What creatures can you see?*
◉ *How has the artist made the skeleton seem friendly rather than scary?*

Memories and mementos

During the festival, families make an *ofrenda* – an altar on which they arrange photos, goods, clothes and favourite foods of the dead person. They decorate the altar with candles, skulls made of sugar or papier mâché (*see top right image*), funny skeletons, marigolds and bright paper cut-outs.

◉ *How did the artist make this skull a symbol of both life and death?*

Papier Mâché Skull
David Moctezuma
2003 (20 cm high)

Silly skeletons

Some artists make scenes of comical clay skeletons, dressed in clothes and doing everyday things – dancing, riding bicycles, watching television or playing music, for example.

◉ *What is strange about the two skeletons below?*

Skeleton Couple, *José Vara, 2003 (55 cm high)*

SCULPTED SKELETONS

Bouncing bones

Make a friendly model skeleton.

◉ Using self-hardening clay, mould a skull, ribcage, pelvis, thigh, shin, upper arm and forearm bones separately. Look at a book on the body for reference.

◉ While the clay is soft, pierce holes – with a fat needle – through the points where one bone will be joined to another.

◉ Leave the clay to harden, then paint it white and add markings.

◉ Join the bones by threading thin wire through the holes and twisting the wire ends together.

◉ Hang your skeleton up.

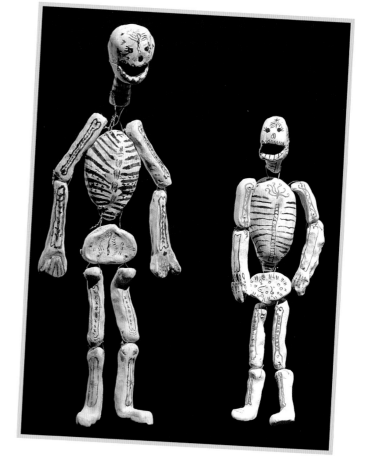

Made in art club, by children aged 8-11

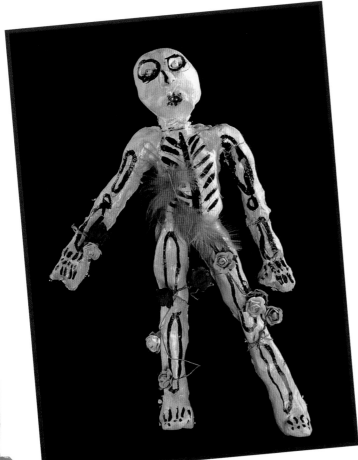

A sprouting skeleton

◉ Make a clay skeleton, all in one piece. Make dents for facial features.

◉ Once the clay has hardened, paint it and then stick on feathers, paper flowers and leaves for decoration.

Picture hunt

✧ Look at the skeletons in black and-white prints by José Guadalupe Posada.

✧ Compare scary images such as James Ensor's **Skeletons Warming Themselves** and **Skeletons in the Studio**, or **The Dance of Death** by Hans Holbein.

Josie, aged 9

Funnybones

Sculpt an ordinary human figure with a skull.

◉ Shape your figure in self-hardening clay.

Christina, aged 11

Charlotte, aged 11

◉ When the clay has dried and hardened, paint the figure in cheerful, bright colours.

◉ Make several figures to arrange in a scene, just as Mexican artists do. How about a band of musicians, market stalls or a wedding party?

Sophie, aged 8, Charlotte, aged 10, and Stephanie, aged 11

Louise, aged 11

Lauren, aged 11

Charlotte, aged 11

Spooky skulls

Model a bony skull paperweight.

◉ Roll out a piece of self-hardening clay, until it is about 2.5 cm thick.

◉ Cut out a skull shape.

◉ Poke holes, or make dents, for the eyes and mouth. Mould a nose.

◉ Leave the clay to dry, then paint it white with spooky black patterns.

ARTISTS AND ANSWERS

TIME TO CELEBRATE (pages 4/5)

ABOUT MARC CHAGALL

Chagall (1887-1985) was born in Russia. He studied art in St Petersburg and then in Paris. As well as painting, he designed stage sets and illustrated books. During World War II, he fled to America. He later returned to France and created huge murals and tapestries.

ABOUT CLAUDE MONET

Monet (1840-1926) grew up on the north coast of France. A local artist encouraged him to paint out in the open air, instead of indoors in a studio as most other artists did. Monet then moved to Paris and befriended other artists, such as Alfred Sisley, Pierre-Auguste Renoir and Camille Pissarro. He persuaded them to paint outdoors as well. They developed a style known as Impressionism, named after one of Monet's paintings.

WELCOME TO THE WORLD (pages 6/7)

Answers for pages 6 and 7

• *The two women are sisters.*
• *Their eyes are different colours; their necklaces are different; the patterns on their sleeves, dress fronts and the lace inside their ruffs (large collars) are all different. The right-hand woman holds her baby more tightly than her sister does.*
• *It is strange that the two sisters are sharing a bed, and that they are sitting in it fully clothed.*
• *The patterns on the babies' christening robes match the patterns of their mothers' dress fronts.*
• *The main colours are red, white and black.*
• *The red shawls frame the babies and make them stand out, emphasising that they are the most important part of the picture.*

ABOUT 17TH-CENTURY BRITISH PAINTING

The artist of this painting is unknown, because painters of the time rarely signed their pictures. Painters were considered craftsmen, like gilders and woodcarvers. They were members of a guild – a society that decided how they did their work. They painted in workshops, run by a master who employed several assistants and trained apprentices. Everyone in the workshop had a different role. The apprentices ground colours for paint; the master painted the most important parts of a picture and the assistants filled in the details

FEASTING AND FUN (pages 10/11)

Answers for pages 10 and 11

• *The person dressed as St George is on a horse in front of the church, riding towards a man pushing a dummy dragon on wheels.*
• *St George appears on the banner by the inn on the far right of the picture.*
• *Apart from those having fun, there are people quarrelling, feeling ill and being tugged by a dog.*
• *The church and the inn are the most important buildings.*
• *The windmill on the hill, which ground the villagers' wheat into flour, is the clue that the villagers farmed.*
• *The banner of St George and the fabric of the stage surround are both red.*

ABOUT ABEL GRIMMER

Grimmer (c1570-1619) lived in Antwerp (now in Belgium). His father Jacob was also a painter and their styles are very similar. Grimmer painted mainly landscapes and pictures of everyday life, full of lively and amusing details.

LET THERE BE LIGHT (pages 14/15)

Answers for page 15

• *Dufy symbolises the world by showing famous monuments and landmarks from different countries. See how many you can recognise.*

• The named figures are: Ferrié, Edison, Graham Bell, Pierre Curie, Marie Curie, Hertz, Moseley, H. A. Lorentz, Hittorff, Mendeleieff and H. Poincaré.
• Dufy has painted the overall wash of the background in deep colours, so the lights stand out in bright contrast.

ABOUT RAOUL DUFY

Dufy (1877-1953) grew up in the French port of Le Havre and then moved to Paris. There, he was influenced by the artist Henri Matisse, who used unusually strong colours in his work. Dufy developed his own bright, sketchy style. He painted light-hearted, sunny scenes of the seaside town of Nice, as well as regattas (boat races) and horse races. He also illustrated books and designed fabrics and ceramics.

A GLORIOUS GOAL (pages 18/19)

Answers for pages 18 and 19

• The goal scorer looks determined and is concentrating hard. He looks as if he has only just kicked the ball, whereas his team mates are already celebrating his goal.
• The losers look disappointed, unhappy and crushed. The goalkeeper and the player in the centre are hunched up; one player has fallen to the ground and another looks off-balance, as if he is about to fall as well. None of the losers looks at any of the others; most of them look downwards.
• The losing team's colours are black and blue, which feel sad, while the winners wear bright, happy yellow and pink.
• Roberts may have added extra lines and goal-posts to give the picture a greater feeling of all-over movement, or to emphasise the importance of the goal.
• The photographers add to the excitement of the moment. They are each trying to capture the best shot of the goal in very different poses – standing, kneeling and lying down.

ABOUT WILLIAM ROBERTS

Roberts (1895-1980) was an English artist who trained at London art schools and became a founder of English Cubism (known as Vorticism). During World War I, he was a war artist for the Canadians, recording front line battles. He is known mainly for pictures of everyday life in London – including scenes of horse racing, boxing, sunbathing, dining and moving house. His solid, simple, tubular figures are very distinctive.

CARNIVAL PARADE
(pages 22/23)

Answers for pages 22 and 23

• The costume's patterns are mainly geometric and the colours match the head-dress, giving a feeling of harmony.
• The bird's huge eye and beak are more noticeable at first than the mask.
• The face mask curves out from the bird's neck, doubling as its puffed-out chest.
• The fabric flaps look like feathers.

ABOUT CARNIVAL

Carnival is held just before Lent – a period when Christians used to give up meat (carne vale means 'farewell meat' in Italian). It is a time for celebrating things that people often take for granted.

A DAY FOR THE DEAD (pages 26/27)

Answers for page 27

• There is a lizard, a caterpillar, a bird and a grasshopper-like insect.
• The big eyes and teeth, the wide smile and the jaunty pose all create a friendly feel.
• The signs of death are sunken eye sockets, huge teeth and no nose or hair. The signs of life are leafy patterns, and flowers in place of eyes.
• The skeletons have hair and eyebrows.

ABOUT FELIPE LINARES

Linares (b.1936) learned his skills from his father Pedro, a well-known creator of papier mâché monsters. Felipe now works with his own two sons. They recently created figures of the Seven Deadly Sins for a museum in Scotland.

ABOUT DAVID MOCTEZUMA

Moctezuma is a Mexican artist who works in papier mâché, making Day of the Dead figures and fantastic monsters, inspired by those of the Linares family.

ABOUT JOSÉ VARA

Vara and his family live in Metepec, west of Mexico City. He specialises in making playful clay figures and Trees of Life (sculptures covered with flowers, birds, and Biblical figures such as Adam and Eve). His daughter Emilia paints many of his models.

GLOSSARY

apprentice A trainee who works for a skilled person, in order to learn how to do his or her job or craft.

collage A picture made by sticking bits of paper, fabric, or other objects, on to a background.

composition The way the subject of a picture, photograph or other artwork is arranged.

Cubism A 20th-century art style in which artists broke down subjects into geometric shapes.

Impressionism An art movement in which artists painted outdoors, focusing on the effects of light.

mural A picture painted to cover a wall.

pose A physical position, or the action of getting into a position deliberately eg posing for a photo.

symbol A picture, or other kind of image, that stands for something else.

texture How something feels to the touch, eg rough or smooth.

INDEX